Structure: the essence of architecture

Architecture is a logical art and that logic is founded on structural principles. It is impossible to understand architecture without an appreciation of the human response to the strength of materials and the structural geometries that balance huge weights in the air against the pull of gravity.

We humans experience an atavistic perceptual response to the control of structural forces. We are conscious of the space membrane between columns and the spatial sanctuary around them. We emphasize with the vertical integrity of the column, the compressive strength of the arch, the tenuous ductility of the cable.

Architecture is all too often described in terms of the fine arts, painting, music and sculpture, but the definition of architecture is 'the art of building'. The pleasure to be found in architecture is the perceptual response felt in the presence of controlled structural forces.

This book describes architecture for what it is – a structural art. It tells of the principles of structure in terms of our perceptual response to them. Its purpose is not to teach architectural engineering or art appreciation, but to stimulate a vital response to the art of building.

Forrest Wilson AIA is the former editor of *Progressive Architecture,* now director of the School of Architecture, Design and Planning, Ohio University, Athens, Ohio. He has practised as an architect, had two one-man shows in New York, and taught at Pratt Institute, Brooklyn, the Parsons School of Design New York and at San Carlos, Mexico City. He is the author of a number of books on architecture and building.

Structure: the essence of architecture

Forrest Wilson

Studio Vista: London
Van Nostrand Reinhold Company: New York

A Studio Vista/Van Nostrand Reinhold Paperback
Edited by John Lewis
First published in London 1971 by Studio Vista
Blue Star House, Highgate Hill, London N19
and in New York by Van Nostrand Publishing Company
a Division of Litton Educational Publishing Inc.
450 West 33 Street, New York, NY 10001
Library of Congress Catalog Card Number: 77-161972
Set in 11/12 pt Baskerville
Printed and bound in the Netherlands
by Drukkerij Reclame N.V., Gouda
ISBN 0 289 70239 9 (paperback)
      0 289 70240 2 (hardback)

CONTENTS

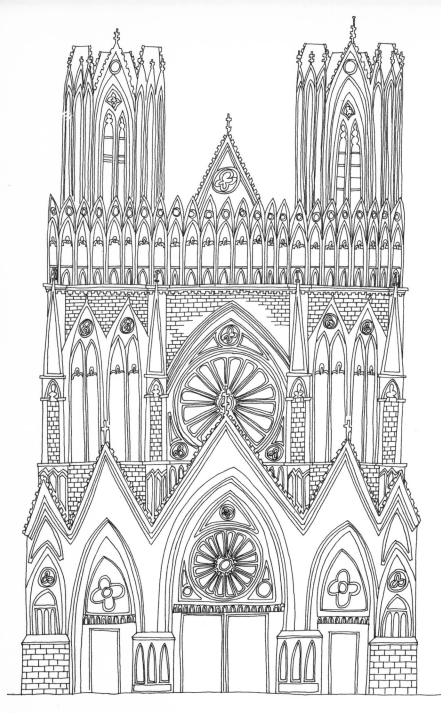

Before men had power saws, automatic hammers and all the machinery we now have to cut wood into boards and stone into blocks, they believed that rocks and trees had souls. Ancient builders worked their building material carefully, begged the stone's forgiveness when they removed him from the ground and asked the tree's pardon for thinning her branches. When buildings were built by hand, cornerstones were laid with ceremony, thresholds were blessed and the spirit of the building revered.

Today we have a great deal of machinery to help us assemble buildings, huge cranes that lift entire sections of the building into the air and trucks that carry enough concrete in one load to build a small house. But it takes more than putting building materials together to create architecture. No one can explain exactly what that more is, except that architecture has a spirit and building has not.

Architecture combines external form and internal space, structure and material into one essence. The structure of the building can be explained and the strength of the materials tested, but the spirit of the building, its form and spaces, must be felt in much the same way the ancients sensed spirits within the forms of rocks and trees.

This book is about architecture, it begins with the art of building which man has mastered and ends with the art of understanding our built environment which he has not.

It is a very simple book because the more important things are, the more simply they should be explained.

STRUCTURE

Building is a balancing act in which the architect poises the laws of structure against the pull of gravity. They are easy laws to understand because our own bodies feel the same forces that act upon a building.

We are all familiar with stirrings of uneasiness experienced when we do not understand how a structure is supported. However, if a comparision between our own size and strength measured against the building's materials and structural logic is clear, we feel comfortable. Measurement of structure using ourselves as the measuring device is the basis of human scale in architecture.

It is easy for us to judge the size of a brick wall because we know the size of the mason's hand that laid the brick. The same calculation can be made with all architectural elements. We can guess the size of openings required for a person to pass through a wall or the height of a window in order for him to look outside.

In contrast, it is impossible to estimate the size of a lunar rocket. There are no clues afforded by its smooth machined surfaces. We only know how large the rocket is by how far away we must stand when it blasts off. It cannot be compared to our hand, a door, or a

window. It must be contrasted to other objects in space whose size we can identify, such as a tree, an automobile, or a house. If none of these clues are present we do not know if the rocket is as large as a skyscraper or as small as a firecracker.

SPACE

Although it is generally agreed that building spaces have an effect on human beings, there are no exact laws that tell us the most desirable dimensions and proportions of such space. Spaces are continually designed and built without thought of their effects upon people. Office buildings, housing projects and subway corridors often give an impression of constriction, lack of air and light, by their dimensions. This does not have to be so, the range of proportion between width, height and length of enclosure can be determined and structural systems devised for pleasing human fit.

Human space does not exist until it is enclosed by man-made structure. What we can do in this space determines how we experience it. A room that can be walked across in two steps gives an entirely different feeling from one that requires several minutes to cross. A ceiling we can touch affects us differently from one 15 feet high. We feel the difference although we may not cross the room or touch the ceiling.

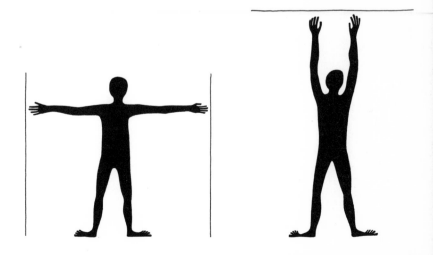

NYC subway *F. Wilson*

Moscow subway *F. Wilson*

Since man moves, space is inseparable from life. He must have space to see objects, hear sound, feel currents of air. Space becomes part of our personal world as structure brings space into human scale.

We perceive space in three ways – by judging the distance to fixed points, by indications of light and shade and by the arrangement of perspective lines. However, each of these observations is liable to error; space is easily distorted by light, linear systems can be consciously altered, and fixed points are not always what and where they seem. Although space is perceived by our senses, they must be trained to accurately interpret what they perceive.

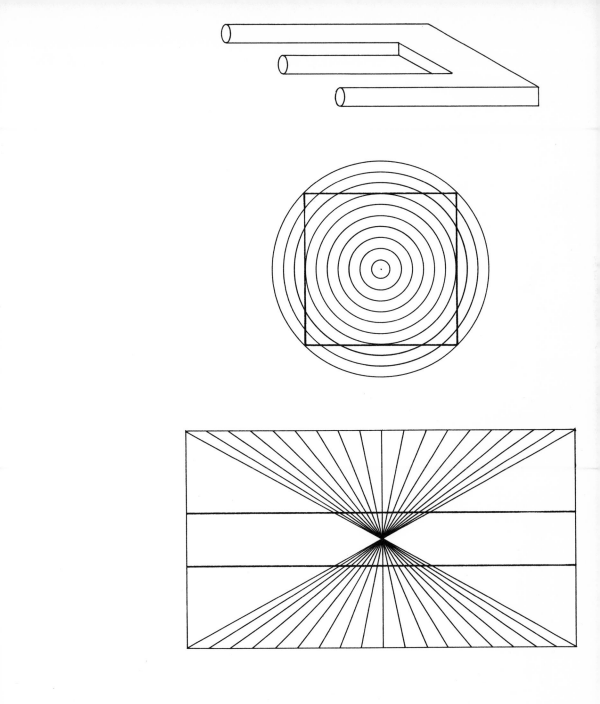

MAN IN SPACE

We can tell a good deal about how people feel about space by the way they instinctively arrange themselves within its confines. Although arrangements differ in various cultures as well as between various segments of the same culture, general patterns are apparent.

There are a number of obvious truths about space although they were not quite so evident until such men as Edward T. Hall, the anthropologist, wrote about them.

As Hall points out, we have different actions for different spaces. We have prescribed ways of acting in different areas of a house, for example we act differently in the parlor than we do in the kitchen or basement.

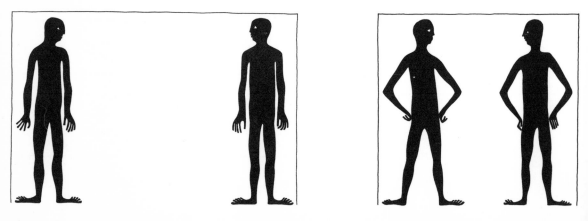

One of our most important feelings about space is that of territoriality. This is the nonphysical boundary outside the physical confines that separate us from our external environment.

It is the space beyond one's body or even beyond one's reach that we consider personal space. For example in our culture, people find it very difficult to stand very close to each other.

When strangers are forced to crowd against each other they hold their bodies still and avert their eyes. People crowded together for a long time find themselves emotionally stressed, sometimes beyond their endurance. They may act irrationally, do violence to each other or go mad.

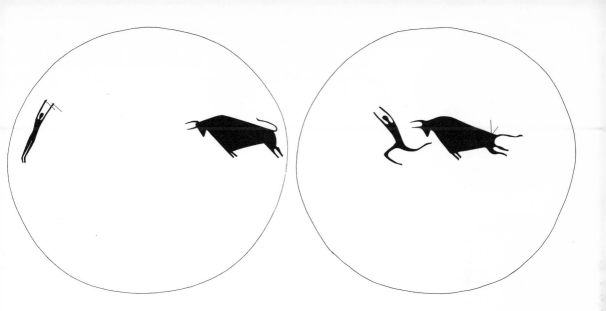

Essential spatial boundaries are not our skins but the space we feel comfortable in. Personal space is essential to us. Dogs choose spots in the kitchen or living room they establish as their own. People return instinctively to the same seat in classrooms and restaurants. Even the fighting bulls of Spain establish territories in the bull ring from which it is extremely difficult to goad them.

SPACE COMMUNICATION

As we grow older we acquire memories of space and instinctive reactions below the conscious level. These memories are associated with unique configurations of space we have experienced. Similar spaces evoke a twinge of nostalgia.

Such experiences teach us that space communicates. Structural systems must be selected as carefully for the spatial messages they convey as for their ability to support the building.

Man must define space. He must be able to return to a starting point. If he cannot return to such a point he cannot survive for

this is an essential condition of social and human movement. It is, therefore, the first consideration of organizing space.

Travellers lost in the desert are incapable of choosing direction because the desert landscape has no landmarks, hence no point of reference. On the other hand it is equally difficult to orient ourselves in the jungle because of an excess of definable points. Man in space needs a recognizable landmark, a sense of place.

For example, we tend to stand in the middle of a circular or square room – there are no orientation points. In a rectangular room there are two axes or two directions, if either of these is distinguished by a door, an entrance or an exit, major traffic directions are established. Two directional lines identify a space, more confuse it, a hexagonal room like a circle is undirected.

For space to speak to us there must be openings, contractions, changes of elevation recognizable differences and orientation points. Endless straight streets tell us nothing. We intuitively want them to end in memorable landmarks; to twist and turn, to hold and release us with a sense of spatial confinement and freedom, to surprise and delight us with new and varied visual experiences. Space, like conversation, must be varied and rich if it is to tell us anything.

Size and space affect us differently when we are standing still, walking or riding in a vehicle. The first, standing or still, is related to the hand or touching. This is the realm of the artist who works close to his objects, creating forms to be touched and examined at close range. The hand-wrought artifact will influence us within a range of about seven times our height, that is thirty to forty feet.

Beyond this distance, the scale of architecture begins. To comprehend the structure and spaces of architecture, the observer should be in motion. A building is best perceived by walking through and around it. The size that can be comprehended in motion, afoot, is limited to about seventy-five to eighty times our height or about 300 to 400 feet. Beyond this distance, even a monumental building becomes an element of our surroundings. This is the scale of the planner or environmental designer. He sees buildings as a group composing one form. To comprehend a city as a single object, we must move faster than we can walk. This is the scale of the airplane or automobile, the machine in motion.

As environmental scale increases, the designer's influence over the final object diminishes. The artist designs and executes his own work. The architect creates by instructing others. The planner coordinates the decisions of others. As planners' decisions are translated into architecture and art, the closer the work approaches the scale of man, the more concentrated and humanly meaningful it becomes.

STRUCTURED MAN

The same principles of construction that hold true for building structure can be applied to the human body, both are structural systems. The human structural configuration is determined by the weight and composition of body materials, the outcome of nature's trial-and-error building experiments.

The human body consists of tensile systems of sinews, a pneumatic system of muscles stretched over a skeletal system of bones in a membrane covering, a beautifully detailed coordinated structural entity infinitely more complex than any building structure ever devised.

Man's size, like that of a building, is the result of the strength of the materials of which his body is composed and their structural geometry. He could not be reduced to the size of a mole nor increased to the size of a mammoth. An increase or reduction in size would require drastic changes in man's structural system. We can do the things we do because we are the size that we are.

As Arthur Clark points out, the world of living creatures is controlled by an elementary rule of geometry: if you double the size of an object, you multiply its area four times but its volume and hence its weight, eight. This means that a mouse cannot be as big as an elephant, nor an elephant as small as a mouse, and that a man cannot be the size of either.

The human structure performs best five or six feet tall. If its height were doubled, the body weight would increase eight times, but the bones that support this weight would increase in area only four times. Stresses would be doubled in intensity. A twelve-foot giant constructed on the principle of a six-foot man would easily break his bones if he stumbled, and a twelve-inch man would tear himself apart if he attempted to scratch his neck. The horse and the elephant follow the same basic quadrupedal design. Compare the thickness of their legs to see the effect of doubling in size.

Mayan ruins *F. Wilson*

SIZE IS NO ACCIDENT

There is a correct size for buildings as there is for man. The limits
of buildings that obey physical laws is critically important. These
laws demonstrate the bond between materials and structural
principles. They determine the limits of architectural structure
and the space it encloses. From them we derive our sense of
structure, scale, and space.

For example, a slab of slate four fingers thick and as long as a
man is high will support its own weight and can be used as a
footbridge. If we increase its size preportionately ten times,
stresses beyond its ultimate strength result. It collapses from its
own weight. This principle is true of all materials, even tremen-
dously strong steel beams have lengths beyond which they cannot
support themselves.

Stresses increase with size even though form remains proportionately the same. There is, therefore, a limit to the span beyond which a structural element of a given material of a given proportion cannot go. For this reason every structural member has a definite proper formal size. In other words, depth to span ratio cannot be constant and is not the same for a short span as it is for a long one, just as the size of a man cannot be changed beyond a certain limit without changing his bones to steel.

It is also true that a given section cannot be decreased to less than its structural necessities. If the builder is guided by structurally derived laws of proportion alone, form can be abstracted only within a certain range.

This does not mean that structural forms derived from physical laws will not have great variety. In any given set of circumstances, the designer will find a number of structural means, equally efficient, to enable him to exercise his aesthetic preferences. There are an infinite number of structurally correct forms for every building, just as there are an infinite variety of fish adapting to the pressures of the ocean depths and of birds supporting themselves on thin currents of air.

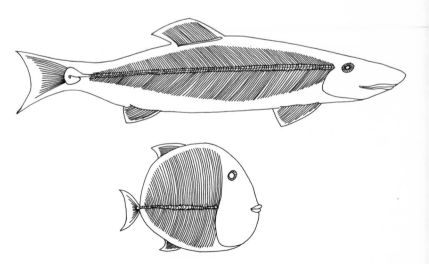

The function of building structure, in the simplest terms, is to hold the building up. It does this by supporting building loads against the pull of gravity. Structures must also be strong enough to resist wind pressures, shock waves, sonic booms, vibrations, physical impact loads and earthquakes. As the result of designing for these possibilities as much as seventy per cent of the building's strength is needed to withstand forces that may never be applied, or if they do occur will only affect the building for a very short period of time. Thus the major portion of the structure is designed for emergency rather than normal conditions.

Besides these stresses, the designer must consider the nature of the materials themselves. These may deteriorate or dimensions may alter with time. For example, seemingly solid, durable concrete expands when hot and contracts when it cools, increases in size when wet and shrinks in drying, under a constant pressure of applied loads it will slowly creep in dimension or sag out of shape.

Each building material acts differently under different conditions yet all materials have qualities in common. They have distinct properties of strength, stiffness, hardness, corrosion resistance, and aging that although varying in magnitude, can be measured on a common scale of stress, strain and deformation. As a consequence, we are able to predict material behavior and to design structures using a variety of materials combined into one building.

One of the most important aspects of material behavior is that of deformation under stress. Although deformation is sometimes so small that is can only be detected by delicate measuring instruments, it is always present.

Elastic materials have a proportionate relationship between force and deformation. For example, if two tons of weight attached to the end of a steel rod caused it to lengthen one sixteenth of an inch, four tons will increase the deformation to one eighth, six tons to three eighths, and so on; deformation is measured in direct proportion to stress. However, there is a 'yield point' at which the material will deform out of proportion to the stress exerted upon it. It might support more weight beyond this point before breaking, but, it is no longer trustworthy because its deformation is no longer predictable.

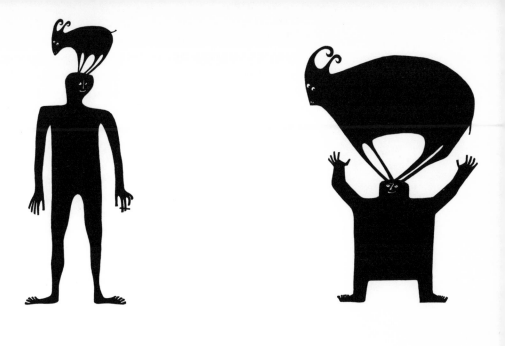

The kind of stress, whether compressive or tensile, is also critically important. For example, metals and woods can be almost as strong in tension as they are in compression. However, brick, concrete and stone have very little tensile strength; therefore, structures of brittle materials must be designed so that maximum value is obtained from their compressive strength while subjecting them to as little tension as possible.

Little skill is required to design a building that will stand up. The pyramids, for example, were never allowed the choice of falling down. An unlimited number of structural configurations will support a building. The selection of the best one may depend upon economics, time and other factors unrelated to structural purity. However, for our purpose, we will speak of ideal structural solutions which means a minimum of material used to obtain maximum results.

OPTIMIZATION

The word used to express this principle is optimization. For illustration we can use the spacing of bridge piers over a lake.

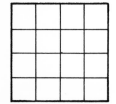

Pier cost will be lowest with the least number of piers at the greatest distance. But as pier costs decrease, the cost of the deck spans, as they become longer and larger between the piers, is increased. At some spacing, pier and deck costs combined will be minimal. This is the optimum of the system. Obviously, the optimum use of piers depends upon the efficiency of the deck span. Similarly if we wish to enclose a maximum square footage of building area with a minimum of linear wall construction, we must select the appropriate geometric figure to accomplish this. In a rectilinear system, the square is the obvious solution. If you will count the squares representing square foot area within each of the adjacent figures, you will find the square encloses the greatest number. The perimeter length of each is the same. For any given material and building system, there will always be an optimum proportion.

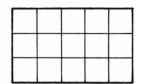

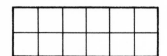

The larger the enclosed space, the more demanding the need for structural efficiency. Optimization becomes the primary goal of design. It is no accident that the ancients enclosed major spaces with the arch vault or dome, the optimum structural system of masonry. Today, suspension, shell and pneumatic structures are the largest of our structural forms using minimal material.

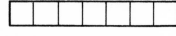

Man and man-made structures are akin, each derived via a process of optimization. Size is no accident. It is the result of maximum structural value derived in material strength of wood, stone and bone.

FORCES

Before we proceed to structural systems, it will be helpful to briefly review the simple principles of forces in equilibrium which is the basic assumption upon which building is predicated.

A force is defined as that which produces or tends to produce motion on a fixed object or a change of motion on a moving one, like a push or a pull.

Push

In engineering diagrams, forces are drawn as arrows showing directions. Their length indicates magnitude. For example, if a quarter of an inch represents one kip (a thousand pounds), $^3/_4$ of an inch would indicate a force of 3000 lbs.

The basic force which attracts all bodies toward the center of the earth is gravity and it is the most important of all to consider in building design.

The first step in structural design is to determine the magnitude, direction and point of application of forces.

Pull

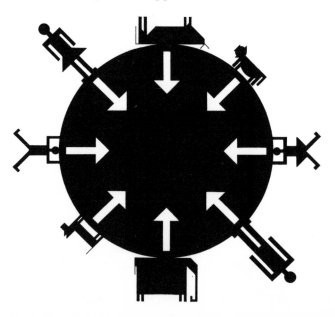

Internal

External

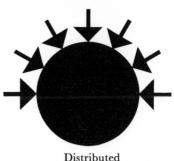

Distributed

Line of action

A force applied to a body is called an external force. Resistance to change of motion or shape exerted by the body to which the force is applied is called an internal force. Forces applied to a small area of a body are called concentrated forces, those applied over a large area are distributed forces.

A force may be considered to work anywhere along its line of action.

When the lines of action of forces have a point in common, they are said to be concurrent; forces not having a common point are non concurrent.

Forces with the same line of action can be added together to form the sum of the two. Forces with the same line of action but moving in the opposite direction can be subtracted from each other. The resulting force is the remainder of the two in the direction of the larger force. Non-concurrent forces meeting at a

Non-concurrent

Concurrent

Addition

Subtraction

29

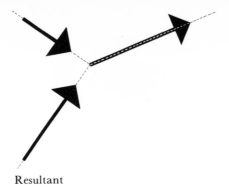

Resultant

point will produce a third force moving in a third direction. When a number of forces are combined into a single force in this way, it is called the resultant. Resultants can be found by constructing a simple diagram called a parallelogram of forces.

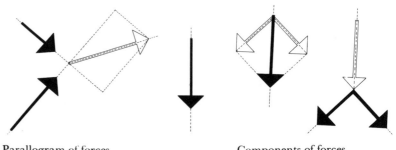

Parallelogram of forces

Components of forces

Such parallelograms are formed by extending the lines of force for the distance of their magnitude beyond the point of intersection, then adding parallel lines to form the parallelogram. The magnitude and direction of the resultant is the longitudinal diagonal from the point of intersection of the two forces to the opposite corner.

Similarly one force can be divided into a number of components by constructing a parallelogram of forces around it. This is important in building for it allows us to counter one thrust with two or more. For example, the force of a sloping structural member may be contained by a horizontal floor and vertical wall.

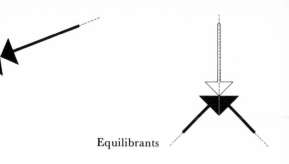

Equilibrants

An important reason for finding the resultant of forces is that if we apply an equal force in the opposite direction on the same line of action as the resultant, forces will be balanced and we will have equilibrium or balance. Such a force is called an equilibrant.

Forces that act in the same or opposite direction but not in the same line of action are non-concurrent parallel forces. These are typified by loads on a horizontal beam. Parallel forces in opposite directions tend to rotate around each other.

The see-saw is a simple example of the principle of parallel forces. If the board is to remain motionless, the distance times weight of each occupant must be equal.

If the see-saw principle is reversed, we have two columns and a beam with a load in the middle. To find the magnitude of stress working on any given section of a beam, we simply measure the

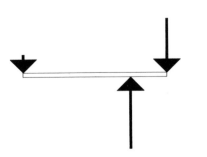

magnitude of the force times the distance to that point, which brings us to the term, moment.

The moment of a force is defined as the tendency of a force to cause rotation about a given point or axis. If we know the direction of the force and the given point, we can easily determine whether it will cause a clockwise or counterclockwise moment. If we know the magnitude of the force and its distance from the point, we can, by multiplying the two, determine the magnitude of the moment.

Forces acting on a body in opposite directions, not in the same line of action, form a mechanical couple. The operation of an automobile steering wheel is an example. One hand will move up and the other down to turn the wheel. If both hands moved up with equal force, than no movement at all would take place, since the forces would equalize each other.

If we consider forces acting on a beam supported by columns, the force in the middle tends to move down. The columns react by pushing up. If we look at one column and the force in relation

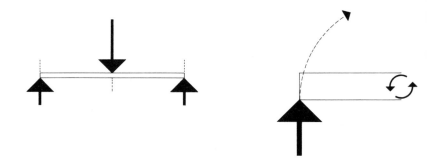

to it, we have a mechanical couple. Its magnitude is the force moving down and the column moving up times their distance apart. Equilibrium is maintained by the ability of the material and the shape of the beam to withstand these moment forces.

Theoretically this mechanical couple is stopped from rotating by another mechanical couple within the beam moving in the opposite direction. The strength of the internal couple is dependent upon the strength of the material and how it is distributed across the beam's cross section. No matter how strong the material may be, it must be such a shape that it is capable of developing a lever arm sufficient to counteract the exterior beam moment.

BALANCE

We know that forces acting on a body change its shape by deformation even if that deformation is very small. Our consideration here, however, is not with this change in size. We assume that if the body does not move, it is rigid, even though it may deform.

The principle of equilibrium is remarkably simple, it has been known and used for centuries. If a rigid body is at rest, we simply assume that the sum of all forces working on it are zero. That is, forces tending to push it to the left are balanced by forces tending to move it to the right, it is being held up by a force equal to that which pulls it down and is being restrained from spinning clockwise by equal counterclockwise forces.

Of course structural engineering involves much more than the few basic principles described here. We have simply defined the nature of forces as an aid in explaining the logic of structural systems.

FRUSTRATING FLEXURE

Straight lines seldom generate great spaces. The geometrically simple forms of the beam and column express brute strength, counteracting forces without delicacy or finesse. The column simply increases its load bearing ability by becoming fatter, the beam by becoming deeper and thicker.

The task of the column is simply to transmit compressive forces along a straight path, through capital to base. If the column is straight the loads upon it evenly distributed, there will be a small shortening of the overall length, but no curvature. However, if forces are applied off center or perpendicular to its length, bending stresses are induced and curvature is the result. Curvature in a beam or column indicates bending stress. It is, therefore, of vital design significance.

The thicker the column is in relation to its height, the more capable it is of withstanding lateral forces and the less likely it is to deflect and curve due to off center loading. There is, therefore, a definite optimum ratio of thickness to height. Subconsciously, we are aware of this, it is the reason we feel uncomfortable near columns that appear too thin for their height and why corkscrew columns are disconcerting.

The structural function of the beam is to transmit forces perpendicular to itself along its length to its supports. If the load on the beam is doubled, the bending forces are doubled and the beam may collapse. If the beam's length is doubled, the bending forces will again be doubled, and it can support only half as much load. However, if the beam's depth is doubled, its strength will be increased four times. Structural optimization of beams is in increased depth.

As beams are overloaded, curvature increases until a hinging action takes place in the areas of high stress. The beam collapses

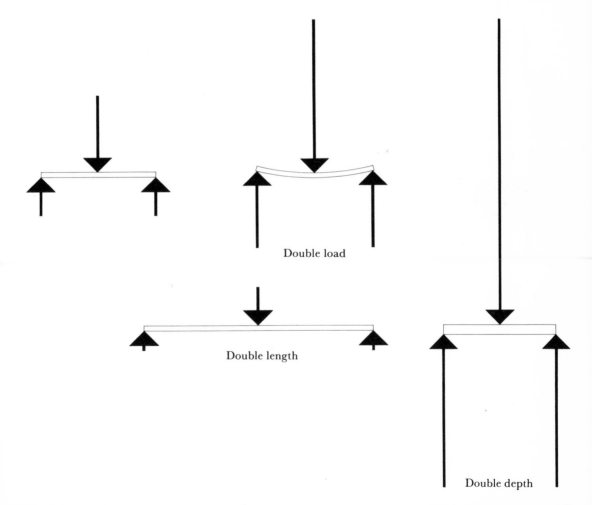

Double load

Double length

Double depth

as though it were hinged at these points. If the beam is composed of a plastic material, such as steel, it will bend. If brittle, such as wood and stone, having little or no yield point, the fibres of the beam simply separate at the hinge points, opening fractures, causing collapse.

The beam and column are stronger if they are rigidly connected to each other. Under these conditions, they transfer stresses to adjoining members, and heavier loads are required to induce failure.

Beams and columns are simple structural members, yet they must be designed to withstand the most complicated loading conditions, that of flexure, or bending. Bending is a combination of compression and tension. Bending stresses are unevenly distributed across the structural cross section. Stress is proportionately greater at the outermost edges and decreases as it reaches the center. For example, all of the material in the rectangular cross section of a beam is not utilized. This is why beams are made like I's and H's in cross section. The most material is placed at the outermost edges where stresses are greatest.

COLUMNS AND BEAMS

Columns are dots in space, in elevation, exclamation points extending from floor to ceiling, horizontal space divisions, creating invisible space membranes between them.

A beam is a dash connecting related building elements, a strong connective carrying loads across space. The longer the distance, the stronger the structural connection required, the more visual emphasis given to the dash.

The cumulative structural system of post and beam is admirably suited to spatial variation. Each set of columns and their connecting beams are, in effect, a self-sufficient structural system. Columns and beams build skeletons, independent of the cladding or building skin. The exterior non-structural surface can be perforated at random for doors and windows without weakening the structure.

Skeleton construction generates a hierarchy of structure with obvious visual relationships. The higher the column, the greater its girth. The longer the span, the deeper the beam. Depth to span relationship can be easily recognized in joists resting on beams, supported by girders, each member becoming larger and

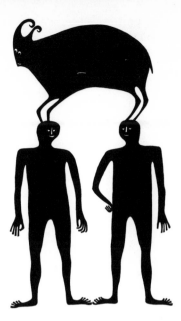

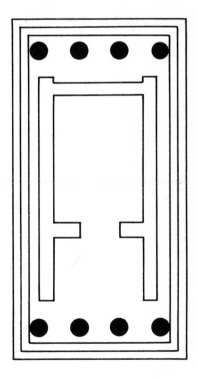

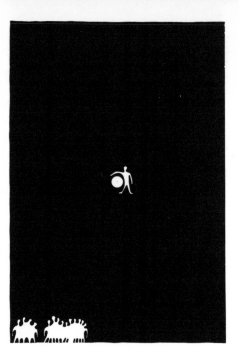

deeper as the span lengthens and loads increase.

Columns offer refuge in space. People who must stand in an open space such as a railroad station will invariably choose a fixed structural element, such as a column to stand beside. The extension of space around the column protects them from the flow of traffic.

Perhaps the most important perceptual attribute of the column and beam system is its accentuation of perspective. Structural lines converge at eye level placing us at the center of what we view.

Colonnades are among the most successful open-closed devices for dividing space. The nave of a church with processional space in the center and space island sanctuaries at the side is an ideal example.

The human mind recognizes space by divisions, great spaces can be great only if delineated. The column does this admirably, it punctuates open space, accentuating its magnitude.

People feel most comfortable with structures they can comprehend. There is no mystery in the functions of the column and beam. The logic of a column supporting a beam at twenty-foot intervals is an obvious reasonable structural arrangement.

The column clarifies the essence of structure. Like man, it stands upon the earth vertically without subtlety or pretence. It can be as modest as the center pole of a nomad's tent or as regal as an obelisk. The beam just as honestly measures horizontal space in its depth.

Cumulative structure is the characteristic of column and beam construction. The possibility of adding elements is unlimited. Covering this simple system with ridged, shed, peaked, hipped, gabled and the infinite variety of roof framing systems man has devised through the ages accounts for the exciting geometries of medieval villages, the New England farm cluster as well as the wealth of forms devised by early American carpenter builders.

On the other hand, the vertical assertion of the column and the horizontal statement of the beam generate the often monotonous plethora of rectilinear geometries which make up our modern urban world.

Machine geometry is often repetitious, boring – deadening to human sensibilities. One objective of designers to overcome this

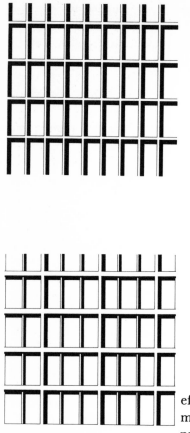

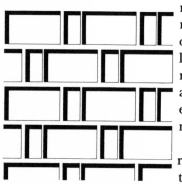

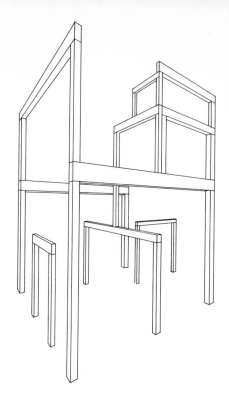

effect has been to vary machine forms within the limitations of machine production. Since the machine is most productive when producing repetitive elements, the design problem becomes one of cycling machine repetition, to produce maximum variety within machine capabilities.

The three drawings shown here are means of changing the repetitive module of column and beam. The first is a constant repetitive pattern with no change. The second shows the frame of the building set forward and emphasized. The window mullions are set back. In the third, the objective was to vary successive rows of windows with wide and narrow glazing. This is obviously a poorly structured wall, for columns that are not directly over each other, offset as these are, would cause severe bending moments, a mechanical couple, in the beams supporting them.

Although curtain wall buildings, because of the endlessy repeated beam and column facades remind us of printed patterns, they are responsible for a phenomenon quite new to architecture.

Lever House at night
Courtesy of Lever Brothers Inc.

When an entire avenue is lined with such facades, it becomes a wall of reflective surfaces – a Versailles Hall of Mirrors in gigantic scale. Here nondescript building after nondescript building picks up the reflections of street traffic, passers-by, and the adjoining buildings, shadows and reflections of the sun and mirrors them in countless faceted images. Nondescript buildings come alive as they reflect the life of the streets.

Compression

At night they undergo another transformation. Lights within give the street an added electric dimension as dull building outlines fall off into darkness while the lit interiors extend street depth.

The pattern, an obvious network of intersecting vertical and horizontal lines, is capable of subtle variation in shadow and reflection. Because these patterns are so common, we tend to neglect their rewarding possibilities.

The boring column-and-beam texture of modern cities, takes on another aspect at the scale of the machine in motion. Patterns merge, change and melt as the eye moves over them rapidly. As the sun moves over these faceted facades, the city becomes a moving pattern of reflective geometric shapes. The buildings themselves seem to disappear. Our cities are for the most part built to the scale of the moving machine rather than walking man.

CURVES OF COMPRESSION

Major spatial enclosures are characterized by curves. The traditional upward curve of the arch, vault, and dome and the downward curve of suspension cables delineate major spatial enclosures. Although these similar, but opposite curves denote counter principles – up compression, down tension – they are similar in optimal use of material. Both the arch and the cable withstand direct stress, theoretically, all the material of the cross section is equally stressed. The most efficiently designed arches have no bending stress and, of course, cables are incapable of supporting bending stress.

The arch encloses space by wedging stones into a bonded compressive cohesion using the pull of gravity. It depends upon the ability of each stone to transmit compressive stresses through

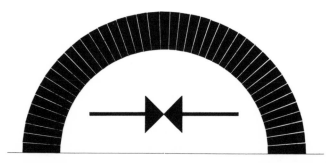

Tension

itself to its neighbors and through them to the supports.

In the vocabulary of building construction, the arch is sometimes called a curved beam although the structural principles it employs are not at all similar. They are alike in that both are linear members that guide stresses along a straight and a curved line to the supports.

Arches, vaults and domes are the earliest examples of the structural optimization of masonry. No better means have ever been devised, structurally or aesthetically to enscribe space with brick and stone.

The theory of the arch can be described visually as we have done here, showing the transition of the components of downward force of each stone into their resultants and transmitting these to the stones below.

Each stone is pulled in a straight line perpendicular to the surface of the earth. But since each is pushed upon by the stone above and pushes the stone below, the straight downward pull of gravity is diverted around the opening within the circle of the arch. To simplify the problem in these drawings, we have assumed that each stone weighs the same amount and have discounted the weight of the structure above.

We begin with the center, or keystone, that divides the downward forces into two components. Each travels in a straight angular line until it meets the perpendicular force of the next stone. The two forces are then added together forming a third angular force, their resultant. It moves in a straight line until it

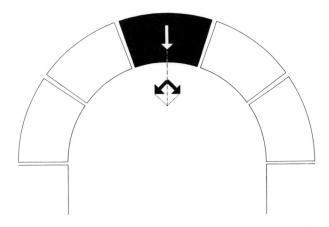

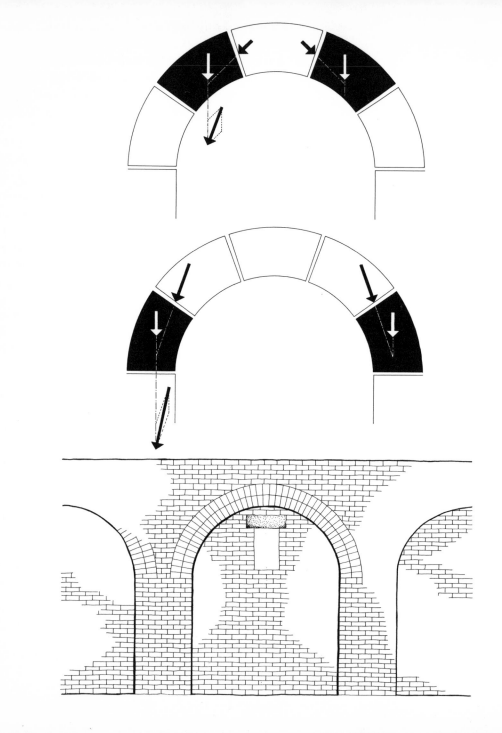

meets the perpendicular line of force of the next stone, and so on to the abutments.

One can think of these angular forces as successively being swallowed by vertical ones until they are consumed in one large perpendicular or nearly perpendicular force at the arch supports. What remains of the side thrust is countered by heavy walls or balanced against another arch.

VAULTS AND DOMES

The vault can be thought of as a long arch. However, when vaulting curves in two directions such as the webbing between the ribs of Gothic cathedrals, it takes on the spatial characteristic of shell construction, which we will discuss later.

Domes are like arches, except they arch both horizontally and vertically. The principle of horizontal compressive action is easily illustrated by two stones tipped forward so that they lean against each other. If four instead of two stones are used, the structure becomes two instead of one dimensional. More and more stones can be added until a circle is enscribed. Then if additional stone circles are added on top of the first, each leaning

inward, eventually a dome will be constructed. Joints between the stones must be fitted carefully so that forces are evenly distributed.

This illustrates the difference between the arch and the dome. The horizontal compressive action allows the top of the dome to be left open. If the keystone of an arch were left out, collapse would result.

The masons of the Near East accentuated this horizontal arching action by laying bricks in herringbone patterns dramatically illustrating the horizontal arching action of the dome in contrast to the vertical force distribution of the arch.

The most difficult problem of dome construction is not arching the dome itself, but covering a square or rectangular space with circular construction.

Solutions to this problem are found in the squinch arch and the pendentive. The squinch arch is a masonry bridge arching the square corners. First an octagon is created, these eight corners are bridged to make a 16-sided polygon and so on with successive arches until the square is circled. A dome on squinch arches falls within the four sides of the square.

Pendentives rise from the square corners as concave triangles. Talbot Hamlin described the form of the pendentive similar to that that would be obtained by laying a hollow orange skin over a square so that its diameter touches the square corners and then cutting the orange skin on the square's sides. A dome on pendentives is generated by a circle enclosing the square.

ENCIRCLED MAN
The eye moves freely in domed space, finding no corners, edges, or axes. The focus is inward towards the center. Man's personal movement is so closely related to the sphere that any experience of space related to this form will affect him as a projection of his own personal space.

The closely scaled medieval interior is perhaps the best example of the rich perceptual dimensions of arched masonry. Vaulting, limited in span, contrasted with heavy rhythmically

47

divided beamed ceiling patterns. Wall perforations were deep sculptured scoops. Sometimes walls were thick enough to enclose passageways, rooms, or sleeping alcoves. Even without furniture, medieval space possessed a rich, formal life of its own.

Massive medieval construction offered security inside of buildings at a time when little security existed outside their walls. A feeling of the times – petty wars, monstrous cruelty, and fanatic piety – is clearly recorded in the structure of medieval buildings.

Weariness does not overtake us in these interiors. We are constantly stimulated by spatial surprise, change of direction, levels, form and rhythm of structure and space. There are few right angles. The unifying form throughout is the curve of masonry. Arches can often be touched with the outstretched hand as one moves through vaulted passageways.

Contrasting with the intimate scale of the medieval living spaces are the lofty interiors of cathedrals which catapult the

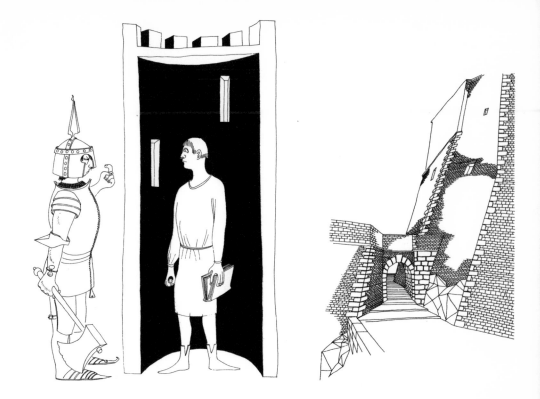

spirit upward through towering naves. We enjoy a freedom of perceptual penetration through space through which our bodies cannot pass.

Freedom that we cannot use soothes and releases us as spatial obstacles, even those we do not have to overcome, cause uneasiness. Medieval masons were masters in creating both spatial release and spatial tension. We experience almost physical exhilaration in the spatial release of a cathedral; on the other hand, fortified obstructions were of brute proportion – as they had to be to withstand the brutes outside.

Space in medieval monastic living quarters, castle rooms, dining halls and even guard rooms bespeaks a spatial sensitivity far keener than our own. We are horrified by the physical barbarism of medieval times, but it is equally true that the monk or half-civilized knight would be appalled at the spatial and perceptual poverty of our environment.

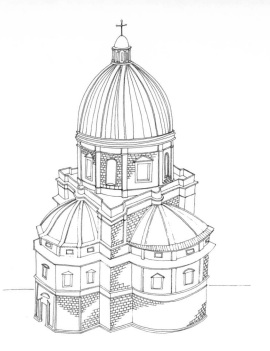

THE JOKERS

To understand the meaning of classic and renaissance structure, one can look at the work of those that made fun of it.

During the Renaissance, architecture was governed by a search for rational harmonious proportions and the logic of structure. In the period that followed architects rejected this rationality. They deliberately manipulated the arch, the column and the wall as sculptural rather than architectural elements. In place of logic, they strove for emotional response. Structural motifs were employed as decorations in defiance of structural logic. The result was a jumble of architectural disharmony. The styles of architecture that emerged were descriptively termed 'Mannerist'.

Often the architect sought to awaken a feeling of uneasiness in the observer: slipping triglyphs, windows within the compressive line of column stress, and the column itself a spiral corkscrew.

Sensibilities were jolted by keystones of large arches which were designed absurdly small and of small arches ridiculously large: columns manfully supporting air, breaks in semicircular pediments, pediments broken and turned in opposite directions.

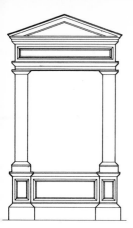
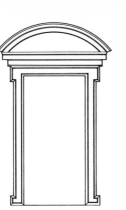
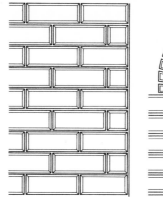
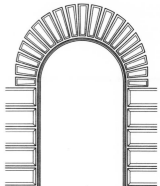

The wall was reduced to a border, a form-limiting, enclosing curtain. Its purpose became the diffusion of light in the interior, free from specific structural definition. The primary material of buildings of the period was stucco, admirably suited to sculpture with little structural value.

Michelangelo typifies architecture of the period. He designed heavy columns on brackets to deride the classic integrity of the column and cut the circle of the pediment to poke fun at the compressive strength of the arch. He played with architecture as he did with the human body, enlarging, distorting and adding architectural elements as he added muscles to the human body in his sculpture.

To those accustomed to the logic of structure and its classic interpretation during the Renaissance, the devices of Mannerism created an intense, vivid, disturbing, confused and irrational impression. Yet, as serious points are often made by witticisms, we

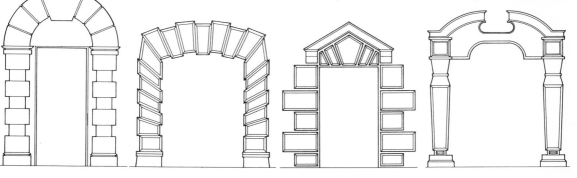

can learn a great deal about the language of architectural structure and its perceptual meaning by the jokes the Mannerists
made at its expense.

The Mannerists were of course more than jokers, although they
often poked fun at the serious meaning of structure. They believed
that the purpose of architecture was to affect human sensibilities
and that structure should be secondary to this objective.

54

MODERN ARCHITECTURE

Buildings that stand because of the pull of gravity and those that stand in spite of it are entirely different phenomena. This affords us a very convenient means of dividing classic and modern architecture.

From the classic period to the beginning of modern architecture, buildings were built of materials stronger than their joints. They were held together by the downward pull of gravity. The result was buildings that used many times more weight in their structure then they were capable of supporting.

The new geometries of modern architecture arose from the use of strong materials and strong joints which transferred stresses throughout the entire structure. Instead of buildings, such as Gothic cathedrals, composed of innumerable pieces and structural systems working independently, the dream of modern architectural engineering is of one monolithic structure with a single material forming walls, floor, and ceiling.

Classic structures were more sculpture than structure. The design objective became the arrangement of known elements – columns, arches, vaults, and domes – into new combinations.

The buildings of modern architecture are the products of modern engineering. They defy the concepts of form and space instilled in us by traditional building. The strength of the material and the joints allow long cantilevers and thin sections creating forms and enclosing huge spaces inconceivable a century ago.

Gravity structures of the past were built empirically. Smaller prototype buildings were often constructed to test the principles before major structures were hazarded. Structural innovation was a slow adaption of proven methods, carried from region to region by traveling master masons.

The profile of the building was modelled. It could be proportioned as the designer felt appropriate since building outlines were not dependent upon structural principles.

Modern building is designed to achieve maximum use of materials. The form of structural members follows the pattern of material stress, with engineering principles determining the shape of members.

Contemporary engineering permits building without proto-

Theme Pavilion Expo 67
Courtesy Expo Corporation

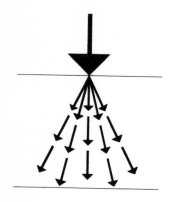

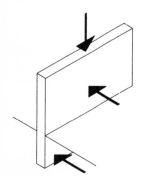

Lateral forces

types. Occasionally models are constructed and scientifically tested with instruments. The finished building concept springs fully formed from the designers' concepts and the engineers' calculations.

The computer allows designers to test the validity of structural ideas that previously had to be discarded because they were often too difficult and time-consuming to calculate. Today new building forms are emerging as a result solely of the computer's ability to test and verify new structural geometries.

WALLS

Of all structural elements, walls are generally the least carefully analysed. The wall transmits vertical compressive forces, applied along its top, to the ground. It acts, in most instances, like a long narrow column. However, the wall must resist lateral forces as well, such as wind above ground and water and earth pressures below. It must also stand against shearing forces parallel to its surface since walls are frequently used for bracing each other.

Walls are seldom built of a single material and are often perforated by doors and window openings. Precise structural analysis is, therefore, difficult. In a simple condition, a large, solidly constructed wall, bearing a single concentrated load, will have compressive stress patterns radiating out from the point of the load's application. The effects are greatest in the immediate region of the load and rapidly diminish away from the point of application. These stress trajectories can be sensed intuitively.

In the region of openings, the flow lines branch over and proceed down the adjacent wall sections. In a masonry wall, the load supported by the lintels can be roughly approximated in the form of an isosceles triangle. If the masonry within the triangle were removed, the opening would be spanned without the benefit of the lintel because of corbelling action.

The pyramid is the characteristic form of masonry construction. As walls come closer to the ground, they must be widened to support the increased weight of the wall above. The ideal wall cross section is a triangle, like the corbel over the lintel.

Walls of one homogeneous material, such as poured concrete, plywood, sheet metal, or plastic, are relatively new in architecture. There are two different kinds of such modern surface construction; the flat plane or panel and the curved surface or shell. In modern surface construction, perforations affect the

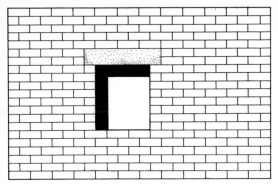

Masonry opening

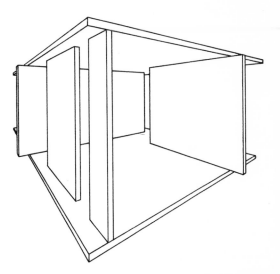

Surface structure perforations

structure differently than they do in traditional walls of brick and stone. A square opening, typical of brick or stone walls built up of masonry units, creates dangerous sharp corners and stress concentrations in a wall of one material. The objective when perforating a flat-surfaced one-material wall is to alter its structural capabilities as little as possible. A number of small rounded openings are preferable.

Flat planar construction is best conceived as the addition of planes almost like a house of cards. Walls perpendicular to each other do not have to meet at the corners if securely fastened together at the ceiling and floor. This is a method of creating door

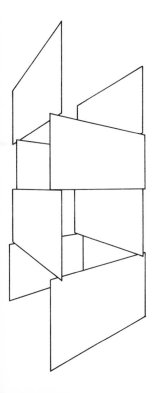

An addition of planes

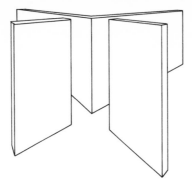

and window openings without perforating wall panels. Openings at the corners allow the planar system to display its unique structural qualities.

Planar systems change the characteristics of light. A window in a flat wall appears as a light hole punched in the surface. If the planar wall is extended beyond its perpendicular meeting wall with an opening at their juncture light is reflected into the exterior surface and brought into the space in a gradual lessening of intensity.

The extended wall reaching beyond its juncture probes space. Such an extension into space delimits a boxed enclosure and brings a part of surrounding unlimited space into human scale.

The characteristics of the planar system are flat slabs, openings between and uninterrupted surfaces that extend from floor to ceiling. Flat planes induce a tautening of our sensibilities. Walled corridors magnify spatial impact. It does not take much distance to induce a fear of converging lines closing in on the occupant.

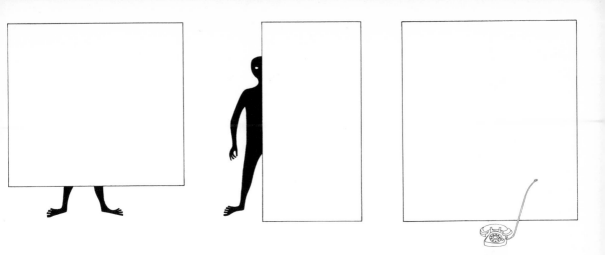

This oppressive feeling of enclosing walls is induced by perspective lines, parallel floor, wall and ceiling drawing together. People enter long dead-end halls reluctantly and stay in them for as short a time as possible. Perspective lines must be altered or identifying elements designed to thwart such impressions if these spaces are to be perceptually inviting.

When we consider walls, it is well to restate the fundamental fact of man's need for shelter and privacy. Shelter is technically easy to provide, privacy is becoming more and more difficult to realize because of increasing human density.

Walls are the first line of defense against the encroachment of noise, polluted air, and exterior visual chaos.

They may provide interior psychological privacy with opaque glass that does not reach the ceiling, visual privacy with plaster board partitions or acoustic, psychological and visual privacy with concrete blocks. However walls are used, as perceptual elements in the division of space or as barriers against the elements, they are the singly most important building element.

TRUSSES AND SPACE FRAMES

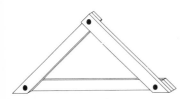

Architecturally useful structures redirect forces, involving action and counteraction within the structural form. If we consider these forces, in two dimensions, we may diagram all structural forms as closed loops or a series of such loops.

The simplest example is the pin-jointed triangle where the

closed loop is composed of straight bars. The magnitude of the forces within the figure and the amount of material required are all functions of material strength and the proportion of the height of the triangle and the length of the base. A change in the shape of the triangle would involve change in the stresses of its members.

The truss and space frame are assemblages of straight members arranged in triangular structural loops. The structural members are designed to withstand tension and compressive forces with little or no bending.

Tension members are more efficient than compression because of the danger of buckling stresses in the latter. A truss designed with as few compression members as possible is the optimum of its structural design.

A span of trusses used as a linear system creates the same hierarchy of depth-to-span as occurs in beams. The structural loops which compose the truss must be larger and deeper, the longer the span. However, when the covering medium is a space frame – a three-dimensional truss – there is no visual indication of major and minor structural members. Forces are concealed in the consistent depth not accentuated by the varied depths of linear members. Space covered by space frames is scaleless, lacking identification of primary and secondary structural elements. Endless identical triangulation creates texture rather than structural theme and variation.

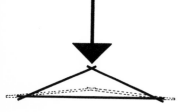

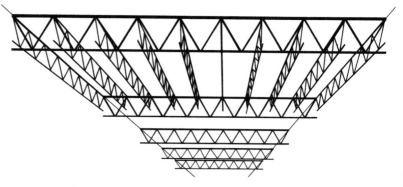

RIGID FRAMES

A four-sided figure with hinged joints may be stabilized by making one of the joints rigid. It can be further secured by fixing all joints.

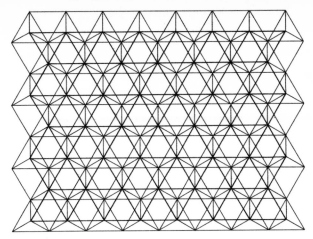

Space frame

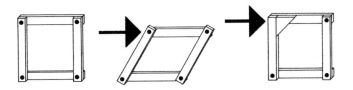

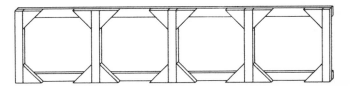

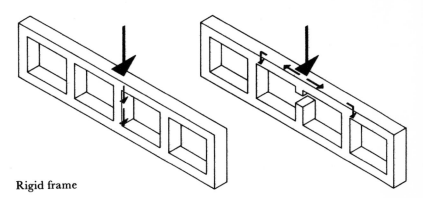

Rigid frame

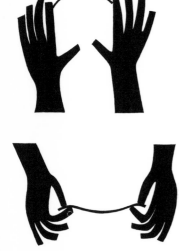

This type of structure, of square or rectangular members with rigid corners, is said to be redundant; that is, if one member were removed, the structure would remain stable assuming no other member was overloaded to the point of collapse. Such a rectilinear truss would reroute the forces around the removed element. Contrast this action with cutting one element of a pinned, triangular truss; collapse would immediately result.

At this point we might talk about statically indeterminate structures which are not as complex as their name implies. To say that a structural system, such as a rigid frame, is statically indeterminate means that the laws of statics are not sufficient to analyze the stresses. Instead, we must study the deformations of the structural elements under load to understand the working of the structure. To do this, we visualize deformation patterns and remember that deformation always indicates stress.

A very simple experiment illustrates the added strength of a rigidly framed member over a simple beam. If you rest a flexible strip between your fingers and push, you will find that it bends easily into a simple curve. But if you grasp both ends securely, pushing up with your fingers and down with your thumb, forming a simple curve in the middle with inverse curves at each end, you will find the strip has more rigidity.

This brings us to the inflection point – the exact point at which the curvature or deformation changes from concave to convex. If the structural member does not have this change from one curvature to another, but is instead a simple curve, it is not statically indeterminate.

Inflection points represent areas where no bending moment occurs. If inflection points are thought of as hinges, then the simple curves between them can be considered in terms of simple bending. Shear and thrust forces must also be examined at inflection points.

The hinged joint allows the transference of compressive, tensile or shear stresses, but not those of bending. This fact allows us to understand the working of a rigid frame. Rigid frames were introduced to building structure with the development of materials that could be securely joined such as steel and concrete. A simple beam and column system rigidly joined is structurally entirely different in terms of stress distribution. The stress diagram is almost opposite in pattern to that of the simple beam

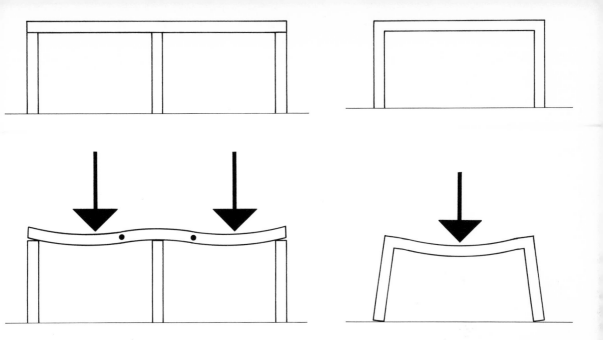

and column.

The terms two- or three-hinged arch does not refer to the common arch that transfers stress stone by stone, but to an arch of one continuous material of vertical and horizontal members with rigid joints. The difference in structural principles can be observed in the drawings.

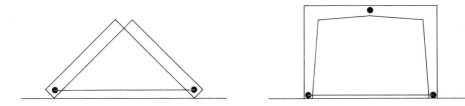

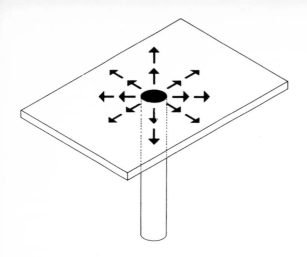

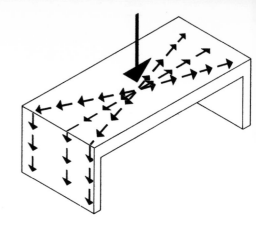

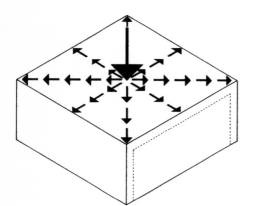

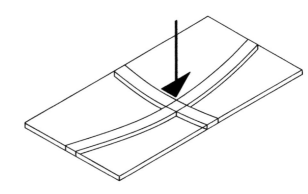

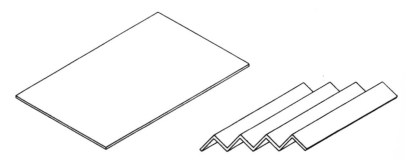

The slab is a flat plate that supports distributed or concentrated loads on its surface. Slabs are more versatile in handling stresses than beams because slab forces fan out along its surface.

A rectangular slab supported on two sides will receive the forces at the supports like a large flat beam, bending in one direction and is called a one-way slab. If the slab is supported on four sides, the forces will travel to each support.

Its deformation pattern shows that a force applied perpendicular to its surface will bend the slab in two major directions. This is the meaning of the term two-way slab. Imagine a perpendicular set of slab strips extracted and superimposed, assuming that each strip is acting independently. Greater moments must be taken by the short strip because the curvature, which indicates bending moments, are larger in relation to the respective strip lengths. Forces flow to their supports by the shortest and stiffest route.

In actuality, a concentrated force will tend to spread or fan out as it approaches the slab supports and some of the force is dissipated in the combined action of shearing, bending and twisting.

A slab may be thought of as a structure with infinite reserve capacities. Forces inside the slab adjust themselves to reach the supports by alternate routes.

Flat slabs may be modified. For unusually heavy building loads or long spans, greater efficiency is obtained by ribbing the slab which permits them to be designed without carrying unnecessary weight.

Slabs can be used as walls or folded plates. The gain in strength of a folded plate can be appreciated by comparing the difference in strength of a flat and a folded piece of paper.

Without the integrally connected column and slab, modern architecture would not exist. The column is left free to raise through the open space of the interior of the building.

The resulting layered, mushroom-like structure permits the independent design of exterior and interior walls and consequent fusing of interior and exterior space.

Masonry, a material weak in tension can be reinforced by introducing a material with tensile properties.

The success of the arch depends on maximum strength of materials in compression. The difficulty is that arches must be curved and man does not walk well on curved surfaces. If a means of placing an essentially compressive material in total compression in a straight line is devised, then, both problems are solved. This is accomplished by prestressing.

Reinforced concrete has steel bars in its tensile areas. One step beyond this idea is the tensioning of steel rods to obtain total compression in the structural member.

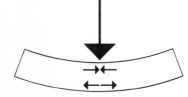

We know that deflection or curvature in a beam is due to bending stresses, that the top of the curve is shorter than the bottom. The top represents compression, the material pushing in against itself, the bottom tension, the material stretching, pulling itself apart.

If this curvature is eliminated, the beam has no bending stress. To do this, a high-strength steel cable is draped inside the beam, when the cable is pulled tight, it forces the beam into a negative, upward curvature. The bottom surface is then in compression and the top in tension, reversing the normal beam condition.

When loads are applied to the stressed beam, it tends to curve downward, equalizing upward and downward curvatures, tensile stresses are eliminated, and the entire member is in compression. Prestressing of building elements was not possible until very strong materials such as high-strength steel cables were developed. Introducing stress to counter stress is a new idea in building, the exact opposite of gravity construction. Prestressing produces a tautness in building forms. Structural sections are lighter and thinner, the building appears self-contained in its structural system.

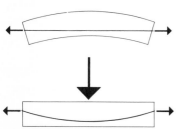

TWA Building NYC *Photo: Ezra Stoller and Associates-courtesy of TWA.*

SHELLS

A shell is a thin plate with a curved surface that transmits forces along its curvature to the supports. Shells must be constructed of materials that can be curved such as reinforced concrete, wood, metal, brick, stone or plastic.

Because of the curvature, internal forces are transmitted by direct stresses of tension, compression, and shear in the plane of the shell surface, rather than in bending as with flate plates. Shells are, therefore, extremely efficient structurally in optimization of material.

Shells can sustain relatively large forces if uniformly applied. Concentrated forces at one point tend to induce bending, which is difficult for the shell to counteract.

A shell counters forces by its shape. The classic example of shell construction is the egg, which, although very thin, can withstand a great deal of evenly distributed pressure.

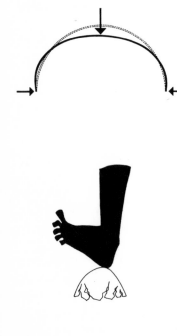

Concentrated loads and restraints of almost any kind cause bending in shells. For example, if edge supports do not yield in harmony with the rest of the shell, they induce bending distortions. Shells must, therefore, be left free to move.

The first man-made shells were domes. To understand the forces induced in a dome, one can use half of an egg shell. If we push down on the top resting on a flat surface, we observe that the compressive forces applied become tensile at the shell edge. It will widen and crack apart. In dome construction, this is combatted by the use of tensile rings such as cables placed around the bottom edge to restrain tensile forces. If the dome is opened at the top, a compression ring is necessary.

There is a great variety of shell forms. The hyperbolic parabaloid is a popular, relatively easy form to design and construct and produces an interesting warped surface. Its popularity is partially due to the fact that it can be constructed with straight members to form a shell of double curvature. Shell design, due to the delicate balance of stress and material is limited to pure geometry.

Since shells cannot support point or concentrated loads and must be free to move, it is not possible to design integral internal and exterior systems that will divide interior space into humanly useful increments. Internal shell systems invariably must be separate from the structure itself. Shells are best used for stadiums, stations, market halls, exhibition halls without interior divisions.

Experiments have been made with smaller shells used as separate modules scaled to human size that can be added to or subtracted from to suit space requirements. Each is a separate structural system in humanly scaled increments that can be added and taken away like grapes on a stem, or units of a honeycomb.

The shell is a seductive form. The danger in its use is that structure becomes an end in itself. Shell geometry is curvilinear but its curvature is peculiar to the structure of rigid materials. Its characteristic is that it is curved toward the same side in all directions, around any point the surface bends away from a tangent plane toward same side, as the surface of a sphere. The strength is in the double curvature bending in upon itself.

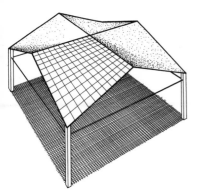

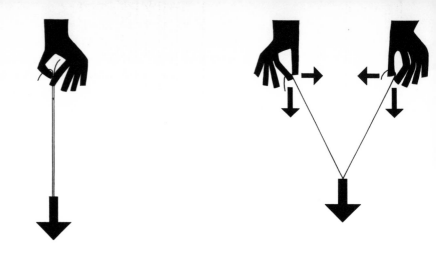

CABLES

The cable is not rigid and therefore cannot support compressive loads nor is it subject to bending. If a cable supports a load vertically, its capacity can be measured simply by dividing the weight of the load by the cable cross section.

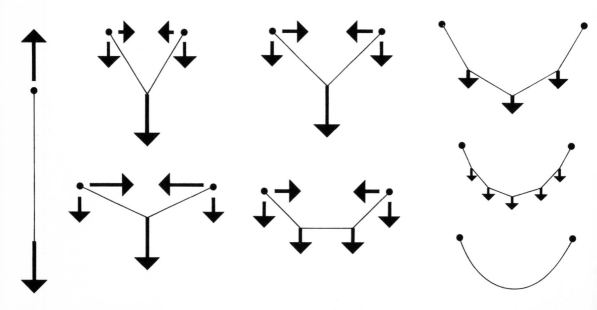

But cables in buildings are used horizontally to support vertical loads. The cable sag, like the beam depth is an indication of how it is stressed. By holding a piece of string between your hands with a weight in the middle you will find that the harder you pull horizontally, the less the sag of the string. Sag indicates cable stress. The strength of the cable must be increased as the sag decreases.

Structural optimization of cables depends on the relation of sag to span. If the sag is very small, the cable will be shorter in length but must be larger in cross section for additional strength. If the sag is large, the cable will be longer but smaller in cross section since it does not have to be as strong. The amount of cable material in relation to the load it carries is then maximum for very small and very large sags. To use the least material to carry the most load proportionately, the sag should be one half the distance between supports, forming a 45 degree angle between the horizontal and the cable.

If the load is changed from the center of the cable toward one of its supports the configuration changes. The two supports develop different vertical reactions but the thrust between them can still be measured in terms of cable sag. If additional loads are added the cable assumes new configurations. As more loads are added, the configuration changes to a figure with more and more straight sides.

If the cable is loaded uniformly along its length, it assumes a curved form called a catenary which can be approximated by holding a chain between one's fingers letting it assume its natural sag. The optimum sag for a catanary in relation to load and cable material is about one third of the distance between supports.

A single layer of cables is adequate to support a building's roof. However, the magnitude of cable sag may be excessive. In suspension bridges, the sag-to-span ratio is about one eighth. In buildings to be economically useful, a smaller sag is essential which means larger than optimal cable cross sections are employed.

The purpose of bridge trusses is not only to support the roadway of the bridge but to give rigidity to the suspension cables. The problem of rigidity is also encountered in the construction of building roofs. For single cable roofs to combat flutter, weight is used to hold them down or guy cables to anchor them to the ground.

When cables vibrate, the geometry of vibration depends upon cable tension. If two cables are used, an upper and lower connected by rigid struts, then when one cable is excited it will transmit its flutter to the other through the strut. But since they are stressed differently the flow of energy from one cable to the other through the connecting struts causes one flutter to counteract the other thus assuring stability.

The cable is the sinew upon which the enclosing material of the building is attached.

MEMBRANE STRUCTURES

Every structural system has limits imposed upon it by the characteristics of its geometry. Beyond these limits, increase in size imposes excessive difficulty of construction and excessive use of material. For example, it is only feasible to build towers for television antennae to certain heights. Beyond this limit masts with guy ropes are used. Between supports, for short spans, a number of systems are almost equally effective, such as beams and girders of various kinds; beyond this trusses and then steel arches are the most effective. To reach beyond the steel arch for the longest spans the suspension cable is used. Each of these structural systems has its own geometry and characteristic means of handling forces: the girder by flexure, the truss by compression and tensile members, the arch by compression and the suspension system by tension.

The cable system is unique in that it is possible to build a small

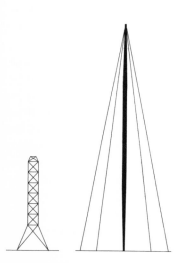

tent of 30 foot span and a large one of 300 using almost an identical geometry, with differences only in size of the tensile members.

The unusual phenomenon of tensile structures is that the size
of the structural system is independent of the size of the span.
They can therefore be enlarged to almost any desired size without entailing an excessively large cross section or change in shape.

Throughout history, gravity has been the basis of stability for
man-built structures. Great arches and domes of brick and stone
have been of such massive construction that the weight of the
building has invariably been more than the loads it was capable
of supporting. With the introduction of stronger building materials, structures have been built that considerably reduce the
ratio of building load to load supported, yet the loads are of the
same order of magnitude as their own dead weight. Weight
continues to be the governing factor that assures structural
stability.

It is only in membrane and inflated structures that the problem of structural weight is reversed. The dead weight of very thin membranes is relatively insignificant and, unlike traditional building materials, does not depend on inherently stiff material.

The advantages of the lightness of tensile structures creates many of their difficulties. They must be anchored down instead of being held up. The problem is to build inflexible structures using flexible materials. These materials with no stiffness must be made to retain their shape under all of the loading conditions to which a building is subjected.

Since the material itself has no rigidity, it must be attained through tensile geometry. One solution lies in the use of a form that has opposite curvatures: that is at any given point curvature is convex along a longitudinal plane section and concave along the perpendicular section of the surface, in the form of a saddle. The saddle and sphere illustrate the contrast of curvatures necessary to attain rigidity in rigid and non-rigid materials.

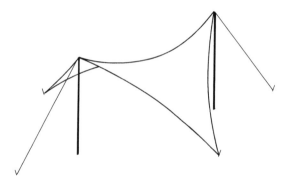

It is not possible to calculate the exact stresses for most shell structures any more than it is possible with membrane structures and cable networks. The stresses cannot be explained in terms of simple mathematical equations.

While it is essential that shell structure stresses by determined with accuracy and that the formulas therefore be as simple as possible, this is not important with membrane structures. It is only necessary to approximate stress magnitude at critical points and the forces acting on the most heavily loaded cables. The deciding feature is to determine the final shape that the desired structure must assume and the forces that produce this shape.

Equally important is the subdivision and development of the surface into strips which can be joined together without pleats or wrinkles, and determining the final length of each cable in the network.

The tensile membrane structure is a pure expression of forces in equilibrium. Its effect is to change all of our concepts about rigidity of structure and counteraction of force with brute strength. Membrane structures use stress and counter stress

alone in naked abandon. There are no extraneous building elements to obscure the sight of working forces.

The possibilities for such structures are unlimited for they generate a new view of the world of structure. Instead of depending upon the rigid circular shape of storage tanks a membrane container could assume an oval or flattened egg-shape characteristic of the liquid it contained. Its outlines would change as more fluid was added and the pressures increased toward the bottom. Such containers could be placed on level ground and need no foundation. They would resemble a drop of water on a polished surface.

The membrane takes on the same physical characteristics as the human body, with inflated muscles and blood vessels, tensile tendons and compressive bones.

The shape is absolutely pure, the result of the forces exerted upon it. A membrane hanging limp is an amorphous form without forces to give it shape. The control of tensile forces against compressive masts give form. The ultimate anchor is the earth itself completing the structural loop. Stability is a function of shape of membrane and the positioning of the cables.

Air and wind structures are forms stabilized by pressures from inside which may be induced by gasses, liquids, foam or material in bulk. The most common example is a child's balloon.

Pneumatic structures are classed as tensile structures. However, they differ substantially from both such heavy hanging structures as suspension bridges and light prestressed membranes such as tents. Their distinctive feature is the container-shaped membrane.

Pneumatic structures are fundamentally a natural, structural form. They are found in plant and animal life, fruits, air bubbles, and blood vessels. The skin kept taut by muscle tissue and blood pressure is a pneumatic structure.

It is man's pneumatically tensioned slightly prestressed skin which enables him to support broadly distributed surface loads. By pressing your finger and then your hand against your arm or leg, you can feel how a pneumatic structure reacts to loads. The single finger causes much more deflection than the palm of your hand as the entire skin surface tenses to withstand the pressure.

Man-made pneumatic structures have developed along the lines of the natural geometry of internal stress. They, therefore, automatically result in pleasing forms.

Pneumatic structures have a very high safety factor. Even over huge spans, the weight of the material is very small. Should failure occur, a long time is required before collapse, since internal air pressure is not much greater than exterior. Even large holes and tears are not dangerous. Loads on the skin of the structure such as snow or heavy rain will, of course, hasten collapse. Wind or temperature differences may delay or completely stop the process of deflation. A small compressor can provide an air supply sufficient to keep the structure inflated.

Such structures have been supported by windscoops taking

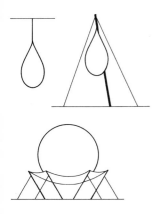

Water storage tanks
Courtesy Chicago Bridge and Iron Co.

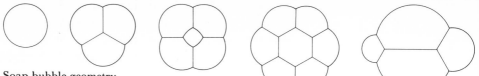

Soap bubble geometry

advantage of a prevailing breeze to inflate them. The principle is similar to that of a parachute that inflates with very little wind pressure. Inside pressure is not sufficient to impede human activities and is not noticeable to even the most sensitive occupant.

The natural tendency of air is to push out in all directions uniformly. If pneumatic forms are to be controlled, they must be restrained by cables, nets, or the form of the container. The formal possibilities of such structures seem limitless. Some idea of their shape may be obtained by blowing soap bubbles or tying strings around a rubber balloon and inflating it. You might even tie a string across your arm or leg and watch how this inflated structure deforms under internal pressure as you move or flex your muscles.

The form of inflated structures and tensed membranes is opposite. Inflated structures curve around their contents as the forms of rigid material curve upon themselves to counteract the forces of gravity. Tensed skins are stretched in opposite arcs emphasizing their emptiness.

The structural standards that normally identify architectural spaces, the weight of columns in rhythmic patterns, the strength of beams, of arches or trusses, the planes of walls, floors, and ceilings intimately connected to the structural system are not a part of membrane structures. Its rationale is alien to our present structural prejudices.

The quality of sound is changed and light takes on a new dimension when it diffuses over the continuously curved membrane surface, lacking the dramatic contrast of shade and shadow cast upon angular building elements.

Generally, the more difficult it has been to build a building, the longer its predicted life span. From the pyramids to medieval cathedrals to today's office buildings, the expected life span of a building has steadily decreased. The pyramids were designed for eternity, the cathedrals for centuries, the speculative office building of today may be demolished in twenty years.

The decreased life span of modern buildings is dramatically illustrated by the fact that a structure is barely finished before alterations begin. Partitions are moved, mechanical systems enlarged, in short, a building changes constantly from the day of occupancy.

In the past when society moved more slowly, there was an illusion of permanence in the greater time lapse between social change and revised architectural planning. This time span has steadily decreased until it can be measured in months instead of centuries. The result has been a throw-away built environment.

Buildings affirm living patterns. They separate social groups, reinforce the prestige of others and distinguish people from each other such as the intellectual elite from the vulgar, the privileged from the underprivileged, the managerial from the working class and most recently, the counter culture from the squares. In short, buildings are used to reinforce the realities of our lives.

In the past architecture has belonged to the elite and building to the vulgar. Modern architecture and good design have been the mark of the better classes since the Second World War no less than a knowledge of antiquities distinguished the 'ins' from the 'outs' during the Renaissance.

One set of architectural realities is represented by today's youthful 'ins' that seek immediate effect without regard for past continuity or future consequence. Technology is employed for perceptual rather than engineering optimization. The objective is not a rational use of materials determined by economic standards or precise or pure design relationships. The construction, material or traditional architectural forms are of little or secondary importance.

'Supergraphics' is a name coined for the techniques of changing perceptual relationships with paint. The box, the cube, the rectilinear traditional structural patterns are distorted in the interest of creating an immediate surface environment. Graphics,

Buildings affirm living patterns

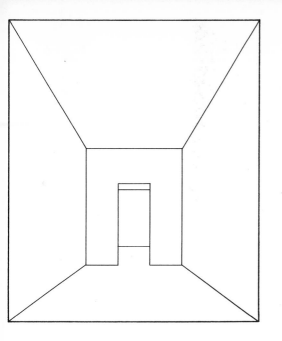

Exploding the box

projected and painted images explode the confines of the box giving an entirely illusory impression of its geometry.

In many ways this is a reflection of the world we live in. Urban dwellers are more aware of signs than the buildings they are attached to. There is more change than permanence in our built environment. The only permanent forms in our cities are the huge cranes on the skylines. We are accustomed to built-in obsolescence. This approach to reality is an architectural extension of what we think of as disposable culture and the outcome of a particularly wasteful system with little regard for human perceptions or even human life. Its governing objective is economic affluence.

THE COUNTER CULTURE
Another approach to our built environment has emerged during the past ten years and differs markedly from any that preceeded it. It has been born and grew to maturity in less time than it took to lay out the foundation of a Gothic cathedral or cut one block for a pyramid. Its purpose is the conscious structuring of living

patterns by a counter culture. Members of the established culture are called squares for the counter culture sees them as living in square boxes, in rectilinear cities which typify a squared cubicled life style. The counter culture seeks to break out of these patterns to assert a freer set of human values, and have found it necessary to create a new built environment to enclose them.

During the past few years we have seen the birth of hundreds of counter culture 'communes' whose members do their own buildings, experimenting with all manner of structures from primitive earth huts and teepees to sophisticated domes and inflatables.

Although commune builders have become remarkably skilled in the construction and erection of these structures, technological proficiency is not their objective. They build to assert a new life style and its sensibilities.

The buildings of the communes have all the attributes of a true architectural style. They are built with skill and conviction and are more than buildings because they have and house a spirit.

THE SENSE OF STRUCTURE

Whether the change in our environment comes from the counter culture or the established one, there is no doubt that our built environment is undergoing rapid change. Building forms without past precedent require a conscious effort on our part to adjust our sensibilities to them. Such adjustment may be difficult for it can defy all previous concepts of structure on which our sense of well being and security depend. For example, people are often reluctant to approach floor to ceiling windows in skyscrapers, yet the same person would not fear to look down between the crenellations of a castle. The thinness of metal sections supporting the skin of a skyscraper, although much stronger than stone, do not provide the same feeling of security.

Today's buildings are not large enough to necessitate total optimization. But as the problems of our cities worsen, the luxury of creating extraneous form for form's sake must be weighted against the desperate need for the shelter of a great number of people. The designer's task is increasingly to find satisfying interior space arrangements within the limits imposed by structural optimization.

The striving for the economic use of material and structural

We are more aware of signs than buildings

Commune builders   *F. Wilson*

The gradual grinding down of man's identity

optimization results in minimal effect. Every line, every angle, every curvature of structure defines the structural optimization of an equilibrium of forces.

Such adjustments to structure and space cannot be made without cost to our sensibilities. We are often warned by a touch of nostalgia as new structural configurations blot out forms and spaces we have been familiar with.

These past associations are part of our bank of perceptions giving our daily experience emotional tone. They have dug their tendrils deeply into our subconscious and are not uprooted without disturbing our emotional equilibrium.

Much of our nostalgia for childhood involves feelings of security in the settings of our early built environment. The healing and restorative power of these associations are retained throughout our years. They afford us a perceptual anchor as architectural landmarks orient us in space.

When all associations of our past environment have been obliterated we are disoriented strangers in our own land. For man to contemplate his future he must be able to remember his past.

As builders become bolder in their experiments with unfamiliar forms, as we begin to utilize all the forms that engineering is capable of creating, it is time to take stock of the meaning of our nostalgia and of the perceptual shock that unfamiliar forms of structure exert upon us.

Almost any form conceived on the drawing board by today's architects can be made to stand by today's engineers. But, structure for human use has limitations, not in engineering optimization but in human perception.

Man is 98 per cent liquid – he cannot be compressed. The futility of attempting to lock people into patterns they will not accept has been dramatically demonstrated by the bloody riots have occured in our inner cities.

The reality of the built environment is more than a design problem. Environment, if not designed to fulfil human aspirations, will either be ignored by its users or destroyed. If buildings do not enliven and enrich human experience, if their structures do not provide human spaces, humans will rid themselves of them.

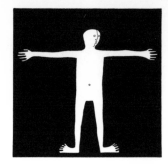

PROCESS-SYSTEMS

The interest of designers in the built environment-in-process sprang from the realization that the only permanent condition of our environment is change. As a consequence the design of any structure is a temporary solution.

Process is a system of thinking that will accomplish an objective with or without buildings. It is a negation of the traditional concept of architecture as the extension of cultural forms with building types.

If the structure itself is not the objective then design must be judged by how people use it, and the changes it effects in human behavior. The emphasis is upon human systems as they affect the environment and the effect of the environment on human systems.

This approach admits constant change in the human behavioral system. Problem situations change before a solution to them can be realized. Solutions themselves are a medium of change, often unpredicted. The task of the designer is not the creation of a timeless artifact or optimal solutions to man's needs. His challenge is to achieve by technical means equilibrium between behavioral goals and environmental change.

Buckminster Fuller dome, Expo 67 *Photo courtesy of Expo Corporation*

CONCLUSION

We have briefly examined structural systems and their relation to behavioral patterns. The objective was not to comprehend all structural systems or to comprehensively analyse one. We sought to explain the importance of the sense of structure.

Building construction and architecture are not one and the same thing. The most significant aspect of structure is its contribution to architectural form. The most important aspect of architecture is its positive effect on human behavioral patterns – not to dominate them but to reinforce and strengthen options.

When structure unobtrusively combines with space, when engineering optimization optimizes perceptual dimensions, then architecture and structure are one. The fusion of architecture and engineering is an ideal to be achieved.

Every line drawn on a working drawing is echoed in human perception. When transferred to three-dimensional spatial enclosure, a structural system becomes a means of ordering, awakening or deadening human sensibilities.

Tomorrow the horizontal and the vertical may no longer orient us to walking and standing. The structural optimization of triangulated loops, the sag of suspension cables, or the bloated puff of pneumatic structures may become the reality of our daily world.

Apartment buildings   *F. Wilson*

When structure is optimized, human options are all too often minimized. The architect's and designer's function becomes one of adjusting engineered space to human requirements. There is no doubt man will have to learn to live within other spatial configurations than those he is now familiar with.

Man's outer garment, the space around him, is increasingly shaped, determined, formed and deformed by technology, with fewer and fewer options in his built environment.

Man's behaviour cannot be completely structured and organized. Such a determination is tantamount to imprisonment. Prison and army life lack humanity, not because they are physically painful, but because man's behavior is excessively restricted.

If behavior is increasingly restricted by the built environment, then the scope of man's natural unstructured behavior shrinks and loss of identity follows. This is the danger in so many of our repetitive, optimized structural systems that obstruct the structuring of the environment on the part of the user of the space.

People do not like to be in places where there is no ambiguity and their sensibilities are specifically directed. The tolerance of people for diversity in their built environment is limitless.

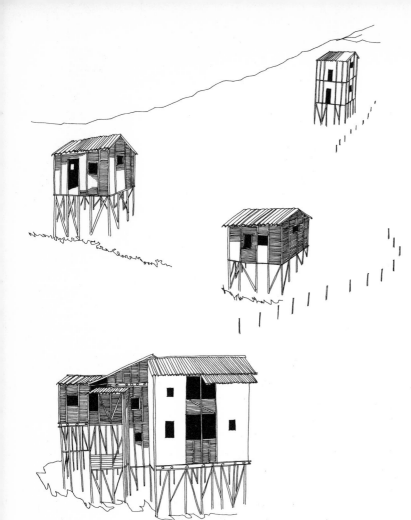

What is logical and rational in structure is not necessarily humanly desirable. Imperfect humans cannot be conceived as consistent machines. Until a computer can be devised to program a 'maybe', it has serious limitations when applied to human problems. Human space must be devised for unpredictable human

beings, not for programmed mechanically consistent automatons.

The rational approach to structuring human space must include all elements of human reaction to it even if these elements prove to be irrational. Spontaneous human reactions must be allowed dimension.

The gradual technical grinding down of man's identity can be countered by allowing him to structure his own behavior in the built environment. The best instrument for accomplishing this is man himself. If the infinite variety of human experience, perception, and inventiveness can be encouraged within the structural system, then the core of man's sensibilities, his basic freedom, can exert itself.

For the man-made environment to be a source of never ending learning, and sensual and perceptual stimulation, structures must be structurally useful and perceptually stimulating. We are now painfully aware from our present surroundings that these needs cannot be met by the professional designer alone.

If our built environment is to have the spirit of architecture, that spirit must come from the users. We are all users.